WHY WE FIGHT

Soldiers, Sailors, Airmen and Marines
Talk About America, Service, Family and Freedom

By **L. Douglas Keeney**
Author **The Eleventh Hour**

**Bulk orders and quantity discounts available.
Special editions, which include personalized
covers, government agency imprints, and
corporate imprints, are available in quantity.
For more information, please see
http://douglaskeeney.com/contact.**

All photos courtesy: The Department of Defense,
The Central Intelligence Agency, or the National
Archives, unless otherwise noted.

Library of Congress Cataloging-in-Publication
Data Available.

ISBN: 978-0-578-36251-9

DEDICATION

Dedicated to Murph, Piggy, Ditch, Gundawg, Jet, Sherm, Skate, Cosmos,
and the countless soldiers, sailors, airmen, and marines who shared their stories
with me as we traveled together, had a beer or attended ceremonies.
They served. They sacrificed. They were dedicated to freedom.

"Veterans know better than anyone else the price of freedom, for they've suffered the scars of war. We can offer them no better tribute than to protect what they have won for us."

- Ronald Reagan

A young woman welcomes an American serviceman with a bouquet of flowers during a 1960s ceremony in France.

INTRODUCTION

Chief Petty Officer Thomas Ciciora was burned out. A twelve-year Navy veteran, Ciciora was finishing a lengthy overseas deployment that had included combat duty during the 1991 Persian Gulf War. As his ship docked in Florida, he was tired, emotionally drained and ready to get out of the Navy – but what would he do next? Be a carpenter? Go back to school? Ciciora was too tired, too weary to think.

Dockside, Ciciora met his wife and three children, and together they drove through the night to his parents' home in Indiana. As the morning dawned, Ciciora pulled over for breakfast, tired and still in uniform. A young waitress – no more than nineteen years old, he guessed – came over to take his order. "Did you just get back from the war?" she asked as she rang him up. "Yeah," he mumbled as he handed her a $20 bill, hoping the conversation would end there. She didn't move. He looked up. She smiled. "The young lady didn't take offense at my rudeness," Ciciora later wrote. "Instead, she gently rolled my fingers back around the $20 bill in my hand. Leaning over the counter and planting a small kiss on my knuckle, she looked up at me and stared for a second, as if she was memorizing my face. Then she spoke one word: 'Thanks.'"

It was at that moment – that unexpected, out-of-the-blue moment – that Ciciora saw his life in an entirely new light. "For the first time in a long time, I felt like I had a purpose being in the Navy," he said. "It wasn't about money and rank and prestige. It was about raising the flag. We do what we do because no one else can or will do it. We fight so others can sleep at night. And I had forgotten that. It renewed my faith, not only in my military career, but in life, as well."[1]

Ciciora would tell the story of that morning epiphany time and time again. His military service had taken on new life; the encounter had given new meaning to his very existence. And yet, his soul-searching was hardly unique. Why do I wear a uniform? Why do I serve? And what are we fighting for when we Americans go to war?

The inspiration for this book goes back to a program started during World War II that offered, in a larger sense, perspective on why we were going to war against Japan and Germany. The answer seems obvious enough to us today, but back then, it wasn't. For sure, emotions ran high in the aftermath of Pearl Harbor: Movie theaters across the nation played the incredible and, in many ways, not-to-be-believed newsreels of the burning battleships and the thousands of lives lost in the surprise attack. Outraged American boys raced to the recruiting stations determined to get even. But rage and anger are fleeting emotions, the stuff of barroom brawls. Clearly some deeper commitment had to be instilled to sustain that sense of purpose a soldier needs to face bullets and death.

U.S. soldiers board an aircraft during the 2022 Russian invasion of Ukraine. They were headed overseas to help protect the territorial integrity of our NATO allies

[1] https://www.bakersfield.com/columnists/right-words-at-the-right-time/article_57191874-ae76-52ea-857a-9883c6014748.html;
see also http://mail.writtenvoices.com/excerpt_display.php?isbn13=9780743497435

"I felt sorry for the American pilots who had died for us Germans. Only three years ago they were fighting against my country, and now they were dying for us. The Americans were strange people, and I didn't really understand them, even though I had read about them and met them first in war and now in peace. I wondered, as only a child can, what made these people do the things they did."[ix]

[I]   *Capri 1971, p. 326 via Wikipedia*
[II] *Smith, Lyn, Forgotten Voices of the Holocaust,*
      p. 293, p. 295
[III] *Gilbert, Martin, The Day The War Ended: May 8, 1945*
      Victory in Europe, p. 329
[IV] *Quoted in Hitchcock, William I., The Bitter Road*
      To Freedom, p. 218
[V] *Quoted in Nicholas, Lynn H., Cruel World, p. 457*
[VI] *Quoted in McCullough, Truman, p. 563*

Combat veteran and U.S. Army Chief of Staff General George C. Marshall knew this better than anyone. In 1941, General Marshall called upon Hollywood movie director Frank Capra to create a series of films that would explain the deeper and more fundamental reasons why Americans were going to war. "I want to nail down with you a plan to make a series of documented, factual-information films – the first in our history – that will explain to our boys in the Army why we are fighting, and the principles for which we are fighting," said Marshall to Capra. "You have an opportunity to contribute enormously to your country and the cause of freedom."[I]

An American cargo plane delivers food and coal during the 1948 Berlin airlift.

"The cause of freedom." If ever there were a reason to take up arms, it was that. We fight, so said those films, to protect our families from the same brutality and enslavement seen in the wake of Hitler's land grabs. We fight so our families can sit at the dinner table certain in the knowledge that no one's going to knock on the door and arrest them for their religious beliefs. We fight for Friday night football games, the freedom to plow and plant our fields with anything we want to grow; to speak freely, to write our opinions freely, and to move about the country freely. "The true soldier fights not because he hates what is in front of him," wrote G.K. Chesterton, the writer/philosopher, "but because he loves what is behind him." All of which comes down to one word: Freedom. Moshe Dayan, the storied fighter for a free Israel, put it ever so succinctly: "Freedom," he said, "is the oxygen of the soul."

Capra made a total of seven films, each spelling out the consequences of freedoms lost with unsettling images of cities in flames and civilians living in fear. But today, after two world wars and the deadly consequences of dictators well known, seven films are hardly necessary. Today, it takes just one photograph to remind us how important freedom is, one picture of the joy written across the face of a newly liberated child, one picture of a farmer freed from years of brutal subjugation, one image of the drawn face of a concentration camp victim delivered from the horrors of that hell. "I thought I would die, I was [that] happy," said a slave laborer who suffered in Nazi Germany of the euphoria she felt when her freedom was restored. "The sun was shining, the birds were singing, the sky was absolutely blue.... I have never felt anything like it before or since."[ii] A Polish citizen who suffered under the Nazis remembered the day of his liberation, a day that started with joyful celebrations in his village, celebrations that went well into the night. As it grew late, he found his sister, and together they walked home. "The air was warm, but fresh after a soaking shower," he said. "We went via the park, which at this hour was completely deserted. The night sky was clear, sprinkled with stars. In the far distance one could hear laughter and music, but in no way did that disturb the peace and silence of the park. We sat down on a bench, huddled against each other, held by the spell, listening to distant voices, intoxicated by the atmosphere of this night, which promised a new era for mankind, together and as individuals."[iii]

However, without food, clothing and shelter – and a way to make a living – that same intoxication quickly turns into a bad hangover. "The freedom from want is the basic component of any enduring peace," wrote Herbert H. Lehman, then head of post-war relief during World War II. "The cry of nations and their peoples for assistance in the first hours of liberation will present democracy with a supreme test."[iv] Cities had been bombed into smoking rubble; machinery, railroads and trucks lay in mangled heaps of twisted steel, while farm fields lay fallow. and a potato was worth its weight in gold. Particularly hard hit were the people of Holland. As soon as the Germans were driven out, the Allies discovered a nation of men, women and children near death from starvation.

The response was immediate, and it came by air. A Dutch writer remembered the sights and sounds of the first formation of aircraft parachuting food to his desperate nation. "A soft droning could be heard from far off. The droning swelled. The people on the rooftops shouted and pointed at the sky. There they were – scores, perhaps hundreds of heavy four-engined bombers thundering low over the city. The roar of the engines was deafening. The people in the streets and on the roofs shrieked, screamed, shouted, howled, cheered. Never have I seen so many adults crying at the same time. Strangers fell into each other's arms. People waved red-white-blue flags. Everyone was mad with happiness. The children didn't understand what was going on.

First they looked with amazement at the planes and the crazed grown-ups. But then, infected by the crowd, they began to sing and dance."[v] And the relief continued – more formally – in the following years.

"Our policy is not against any country or doctrine, but against hunger, poverty, desperation and chaos," said General Marshall, now Secretary of State and author of the $17 billion relief plan to rebuild Europe in the aftermath of World War II. "Its purpose should be the arrival of a working economy in the world so as to permit the emergence of political and social conditions in which free institutions can exist."[vi]

Therein lies the second reason we wear a uniform, because that war against "desperation and chaos" compels us to stand ready with humanitarian relief, the scale and size of relief that only a well-oiled military machine can deliver. In the aftermath of World War II, Germany was divided into four geographic sectors. Three would become West Germany, placed under the joint control of France, Great Britain and the U.S., while the fourth, the eastern sector, would become East Germany, placed under Soviet control. It was a negotiated arrangement coming out of the Yalta Conference, but considering the conflicting ideologies and conflicting objectives of the occupying forces, it was at best an awkward way to govern a nation in post-war disarray. Still, that was nothing compared to the situation in Berlin. To reach the former capital of Germany, one had to travel more than a hundred miles deep into East Germany's territory only to reach a city that itself was divided into four parts – the Soviet zone, or East Berlin, and the conjoined French, British and American zones, or West Berlin. Here again one found the same conflicting ideologies and objectives. But on top of that, the 2.5 million Germans living in West Berlin were in a very real sense living on a land-locked island, surrounded on all sides by an increasingly hostile, Soviet-controlled country.

Not surprisingly, Berlin became the first major flash point of the Cold War. To protest an attempt to monetarily unify the two halves of Germany, the Soviets, in 1948, unilaterally shut down all road, rail and canal access to and from the allied-controlled half. All shipments of food, coal and medicines were halted at the East German border, which meant that, for those living in West Berlin, there would be no fuel for their furnaces or food for their tables. With a brutally cold German winter just over the horizon, the situation looked bleak.

However, there was an option, although it had never been attempted before. Rather than concede to the Soviets or

Shortages of nearly everything hampered the post-World War II recovery. Hungry Germans cut meat from the carcass of a horse

abandon West Berlin, the allies, led by the Americans, began an incredible, unheard of, theoretically impossible airlift of food and supplies. Through rain, sleet, snow and fog, cargo planes delivered coal, food and medicines to Berlin 24/7 in quantities sufficient to keep the city of 2.5 million fed and warm for nearly a year. To say this was an enormous achievement would be a gross understatement: Flying day and night, pilots of these propellor-driven planes lumbered through the air delivering 8,000 tons of goods to West Berlin each and every day – although at a steep price. Seventeen of those planes crashed at a cost of 31 American lives, some flying directly into the sides of buildings when the city was socked in by winter snow or dense fog. One of those planes came down not far from a young German boy named Wolfgang Samuels. Samuels went over to investigate. "I felt sorry for the American pilots who had died for us Germans," he later wrote of the crash site. "Only three years ago they were fighting against my country, and now they were dying for us. The Americans were strange people, and I didn't really understand them, even though I had read about them and met them first in war and now in peace. I wondered, as only a child can, what made these people do the things they did."[vi]

What indeed?

The need arose again at the end of the Cold War. Years of neglect and the failure of socialism left many of the Iron Curtain countries without reliable electricity, basic infrastructure and adequate medical facilities. The arms and legs of the free nations were called upon, and those peoples responded. Dr. Mircea Maiorescu, Romanian Minister of Health, described an American medical team that spent years helping rebuild its medical system: "Who are these gentlemen?" he later wrote of the volunteer doctors and nurses. "In a short time, we [are] astonished. They are visiting the main pediatric hospitals in the country. They are evaluating the situation, making great rounds, lecturing, teaching, getting to know the Romanian pediatricians. Look, they are doing a lot of things despite the language barrier. We are dumbfounded."

But what of today? After WWII, Russia and the United States, along with Great Britain and a number of other nations, agreed that the rise of another Nazi Germany could not be allowed. To prevent such a thing, they also agreed that some sort of international "police" force should be formed that would intervene at the earliest sign of any expansionism. That gave rise to collective pacts of mutual aid such as the North Atlantic Treaty Organization (NATO) so smaller nations could confidently stand firm against more powerful aggressors, secure in the knowledge that behind them stood the force and military might of the nations in their alliance. That concept is known as Article 5 of the NATO treaty, which calls for the collective defense of the signors. America is one. "Collective defense," reads Article 5, "means an attack against one ally is an attack against all." Article 5 was invoked in 2001 after the attack on New York City and is hanging in the balance as Russia eyes Ukraine.[2]

President Franklin D. Roosevelt best described why we fight when he addressed the nation on the eve of the Allied invasion of Occupied Europe. "They fight not for the lust of conquest," he said of our Army. "They fight to end conquest. They fight to liberate." So it was in 1944. And so it was again in Ciciora's Persian Gulf War. Our soldiers seek no spoils, our nation receives no territory from a war well fought. The flag on their uniforms represents both the humanitarian and the combat missions of our military. Why do we hang that flag from our front porches or face it with respect when we sing our national anthem? Why do we proudly wear it on our hats and t-shirts? It's patriotism certainly, but what are we patriotic about? "That flag represents our history, our freedom, and all of those things that are important to us as a nation," said a rather insightful nineteen-year-old American soldier who was deployed overseas.[3] Said an airman also deployed, "It's more than just a flag. It represents who came before me, and the people I am going to protect."[4] The point is, the flag is a vessel that contains all of our collective beliefs about freedom, family, nation, opportunity and more – as well as the memory of the millions of soldiers lost in the name of protecting those same values, passions and beliefs. This is well known in the military community, and certainly among military families, but far too often forgotten by those of us who live on the civilian side of the world.

Our flag is many things to many people, but it is consistently a tribute to soldiering and to patriots and to all of the first responders who give everything they have when we mortals needed their help. Abraham Lincoln had something to say about that, and it's worth remembering: "Honor the soldier and sailor everywhere, who bravely bears his country's cause," he said in one of his addresses. "Honor, also, to the citizen who cares for his brother in the field and serves, as he best can, the same cause."

Honoring the flag is a good start.

What then about dissent? However woke one wants to be about the flag, the right to be woke comes from the blood of patriots who fought to create one of the freest nations in history of the world. Some people may kneel during the national anthem. Some may turn their backs. It may be unpleasant to see such a thing and offensive in the context of your values, but that is one of the rights that comes with this messy thing called freedom. "I disapprove of what you say," wrote author Beatrice Hall, "but I will defend to the death your right to say it." We can't have it both ways as a people who respect freedom. "This we'll defend," are the words on the logo of a popular clothing company started by vets, something also said by Thomas Jefferson 240 years ago, although a bit more formally. "The tree of freedom needs to be replenished from time to time with the blood of patriots and tyrants," said our second President. We will defend freedom.

Wolfgang Samuel remembered his final steps to freedom. "I am free, I said to myself out loud as I approached the [train] station; I am free. Over there in America a new life awaited me, new opportunities.... over there was new hope. [But] in the end, what I remember most from this journey along my road of life are the people who held out a helping hand, and by doing so gave me a life to live."[viii]

We fight because we want to be that helping hand. A free society creates a powerful foundation. A free society is a place where people and ideas flourish; where ambitions are nourished, and a full life can be lived. A free society is the manifestation of freedom. "The essence of America – that which really unites us – is not ethnicity, or nationality or religion," said former Secretary of State Condoleezza Rice. "It is an idea – and what an idea it is: That you can come from humble circumstances and do great things."[5]

We fight to sweep away the deadly threats to freedom, justice, peace and democratic values. We fight for our families. For our children. For our neighbors. And we willingly stand with those in this world who seek a high place among the community of people who fight for the same ideals.

"First and foremost is the flag patch. The American flag represents everything I and all my comrades in arms serve in the military for. It represents freedom, and it represents home. Wherever I am in the world, when I see the American flag, it brings me home. I imagine it does the same for aircrew members as they fly over Afghanistan and Iraq. The flag and what it represents is why we fight."[x]

[2] In 2022, Russia had soldiers massed on the border of Ukraine suggesting an invasion

[3] https://www.dvidshub.net/news/108574/21st-tsc-soldiers-honor-us-german-flags

[4] https://www.dvidshub.net/news/292590/like-father-like-son-wearing-uniform-together

[5] https://www.inspiringquotes.us/author/1230-condoleezza-rice

[vii] Samuel, Wolfgang W.E., German Boy, p. 368

[viii] Samuel, Wolfgang, W.E., German Boy, p. 424

[ix] Samuel, Wolfgang W.E., German Boy, p. 368

[x] https://www.dvidshub.net/news/50576/remember-why-we-fight-memorial-day

(Left and Top) *WWI doughboys arriving in France, 1917*

"Lafayette, we are here."

On July 4, 1917, U.S. Army Colonel Charles E. Stanton spoke to the French people from the tomb of French war hero and hero of the American Revolution, Marquis de Lafayette. Having arrived just days earlier with the first American troops to enter World War I, Stanton thought it fitting that he speak before the tomb of Lafayette, the Frenchman who decisively rallied the French military to the aid of the American cause. There Stanton uttered his now famous declaration. "America has joined forces with the Allied Powers, and what we have of blood and treasure are yours," he said to the French. "Therefore it is with loving pride that we drape the colors in tribute of respect to this citizen of your great republic. And here and now, in the presence of the illustrious dead, we pledge our hearts and our honor in carrying this war to a successful issue. Lafayette, we are here."[1]

[1] *https://www.pritzkermilitary.org/explore/museum/past-exhibits/lest-we-forget-doughboys-sammies-and-sailors-great-war/lafayette-we-are-here*

"We must take sides.
Neutrality helps
the oppressor,
never the victim.
Silence encourages
the tormentor,
never the tormented."[1]

- Elie Wiesel

(**Left**) *Adolf Hitler, 1939.* (**Above**) *Pearl Harbor, 1941*

"The only thing necessary for the triumph of evil is for good men to do nothing."[2]

- Edmund Burke

[1] *https://cdn.fedweb.org/fed-14/2/MoR%2520Quotes%25282%2529.pdf*
[2] *https://cdn.fedweb.org/fed-14/2/MoR%2520Quotes%25282%2529.pdf*

WHY *WE* FIGHT

"Whoever would overthrow the liberty of a nation must begin by subduing the freeness of speech."

- Benjamin Franklin, Silence Dogood / The Busy-Body / Early Writings

(Top) *A Nazi book burning.*
(Middle) *Roundups of Jews in Nazi Germany.*
(Bottom) *A Frenchman weeps as Germans enter Paris, June 14, 1940*

"The world is a dangerous place, not because of those who do evil, but because of those who look on and do nothing."

- Albert Einstein

The right of any human to live a life free from fear, free from oppression, and free from danger is a basic right common to all Mankind. But fanatical leaders see territory and global domination as the natural extension of political ambitions. Ethnic cleansing remains a dark curse on Human history. More than any other person, Hitler awakened the world to this evil, and to the ever present need to take action. "The tree of liberty must be refreshed from time to time with the blood of patriots and tyrants," said Thomas Jefferson in a letter to his son-on-law, 1797. "It is its natural manure."[1]

(Left) *Concrete hedgehogs at the East German border.*
(Top) *Jewish residents are taken prisoner during the destruction of the Warsaw Ghetto, 1943.*

[1] *https://www.monticello.org/site/research-and-collections/tree-liberty-quotation*

"I didn't like the war, but it had to be." [1]

"Let every nation know, whether it wishes us well or ill, that we shall pay any price, bear any burden, meet any hardship, support any friend, oppose any foe to assure the survival and the success of liberty."

- *John F. Kennedy*

[1] *https://www.dvidshub.net/news/369509/first-army-world-war-ii-veterans-recall-v-e-day*

"We must never forget why we have and why we need our military. Our armed forces exist solely to ensure our nation is safe, so that each and every one of us can sleep soundly at night, knowing we have 'guardians at the gate.'"

- US Representative Allen West, 2012

(Left page) *Soldiers on the eve of the D-Day invasion of Europe, 1944.*
(This page) *Airmen salute as a C-130 departs for a NATO base during the 2022 Ukraine crisis*

On the 20th anniversary of D-Day, June 6, 1964, General Dwight D. Eisenhower returned to the D-Day beaches and spoke to television news anchor Walter Cronkite. The interview was choppy, it started and stopped, words spoken in a reflective mood. Said Eisenhower as he looked down on the beaches: "On June 6, 1944, these men came here, British and our other allies, to storm these beaches. Not to gain anything for ourselves, not to fulfill any ambition America had for conquest, but just to preserve freedom, the systems of self-government. Not to conquer any territory, not for any ambitions of their own, but to make sure Hitler could not destroy freedom in this world. Many thousands of men have died for ideals such as these. But they did it so the world could be free. I devotedly hope that we will never again have to see things such as these."[2]

"I'm a believer in the Constitution," said a soldier who deployed to Iraq in the 1990s. "I believe if I can do something, I have to do my duty."[1]

Left: *Displaced Ukrainians flee the advancing Russian soldiers. Ukraine invasion 2022.*
(This page) *D-Day landing craft approach Omaha Beach, June 6, 1944.*

[1] *https://www.dvidshub.net/news/114936/us-soldier-re-enlists-afghanistan*
[2] *CBS Reports (1964) D-Day Plus 20 Years – Eisenhower Returns to Normandy; see also Ambrose, D-Day, p. 583*

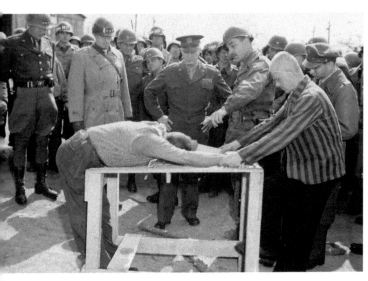

Chief Petty Officer and twelve-year Navy veteran Thomas Ciciora was on the way home after returning from Operation Desert Storm. He had been driving through the night to get from Florida to his parents' home in Indiana. He stopped for breakfast, still in uniform, and ordered breakfast. "Did you just get back from the war?" asked his waitress. "Yeah," he groused, hoping to end the conversation there. "The young lady didn't take offense at my rudeness," Ciciora wrote. "Instead, she gently rolled my fingers back around the $20 bill in my hand. Leaning over the counter and planting a small kiss on my knuckle, she looked up at me and stared for a second, as if she was memorizing my face. Then she spoke one word: 'Thanks.'

"For the first time in a long time, I felt like I had a purpose being in the Navy. It wasn't about money and rank and prestige. It was about raising the flag. We do what we do because no one else can or will do it. We fight so others can sleep at night. And I had forgotten that. It renewed my faith, not only in my military career, but in life, as well."[1]

- Timothy Ciciora

[1] *https://www.bakersfield.com/columnists/right-words-at-the-right-time/article_57191874-ae76-52ea-857a-9883c6014748.html*

(Photos) *Atrocities. Executions. Ethnic cleansing. The electrified fence in a camp.*

Concentration camp survivors show how they were tortured. Russians block roads during invasion of Ukraine.

"Someone is sitting in the shade today because someone planted a tree a long time ago,"

said Warren Buffet in an apt metaphor for peace and freedom.

Time Magazine's World War II war correspondent Charles Christian Wertenbaker wrote of the liberation of Paris. "I have seen the faces of young people in love and the faces of old people at peace with their God. I have never seen in any face such joy as radiated from the faces of the people of Paris this morning. This is no day for restraint, and I could not write with restraint if I wanted to. Your correspondent and your photographer Bob Capra drove into Paris with eyes that would not stay dry, and we were no more ashamed of it than were the people who wept as they embraced us"[1]

Original caption, left: *"Parisians line the Champs Elysees to cheer the massed infantry units of the American army as they march in review towards the Arc de Triomphe, celebrating the liberation of the capital of France from Nazi occupation."*
(This page): *Children are taken outside by members of the Jewish Brigade. Refugees, Italy, 1945.*

[1] *https://time.com/vault/issue/1944-09-04/page/36*

"I cherish the memories of a question my grandson asked me the other day when he said, 'Grandpa, were you a hero in the war?' Grandpa said, 'No, but I served in a company of heroes.'"

- Major Richard Winters

Far Right Page, Original Caption:
"Little heroine to war-weary GI's at Camp Patrick Henry, Virginia. Returned veterans from overseas service took twelve-year [old] Grace Matthews, Manila, Philippine Islands, as their heroine. She had just returned to this country with more than 200 other liberated Japanese prisoners on the *USS General William A. Mann* (HR-286), direct from the Philippines. She was happy to be in America, but memories of seeing her father and 249 other men given the barbarous water treatment (pouring water down men's mouths and noses) were still vivi."

[1] *https://www.inc.com/bill-murphy-jr/17-inspiring-d-day-quotes-to-remember-75th-anniversary-of-d-day.html*

"At the core, the American citizen soldiers knew the difference between right and wrong, and they didn't want to live in a world in which wrong prevailed. So they fought, and won, and we, all of us, living and yet to be born, must be forever profoundly grateful."

- Historian Stephen Ambrose

"I don't feel that I'm any kind of hero," said a veteran of the D-Day invasion. "To me, the work had to be done. I was asked to do it. So I did. When I lecture kids, I tell them the same thing."[1]

"It makes me happy to see the Marines and children interacting," said a school teacher near a Marine base in California. "Nothing is better than seeing a Marine walking on a field with tons of kids behind him waiting to play. Children need a role model in life; they need a person to get them going in the right direction."

"Heroes don't have to be Superman," said one of her 4th grade students. "A hero to me is some who is brave and bold. They just have to want to help and change other people. They are also nice to everybody. It feels good to talk to Marines. It is awesome when we get to play with them. They helped us do the community clean up. The Marines tell us it is hard and complicated to do their job. They always tell us to pay attention in school so we can be good at our jobs like they are. All of the Marines are heroes to us."[1]

[1] https://www.dvidshub.net/news/107131/whats-hero

"You have shown
by your deeds what
the American Soldier
can do when he fights
for a cause in which
he believes."

(Above) *Jewish services conducted in Normandy, France, after D-Day, 8/15/1944*
(Right) *The devastated interior of a church destroyed during WWII bombing.*

Major General Harry Collins, commander of the 42nd Infantry Division, addressed his soldiers as 1,500 of them prepared a Passover Seder in the newly occupied German city of Dahn. It was March 28, 1945. "I am sure this Passover will live in your memories forever," said Collins. "You celebrate it in Germany, in the land Hitler felt no Passovers would be celebrated for at least a thousand years."

As part of that ceremony, the 42nd Division printed the first Hebrew religious text produced in Germany since the rise of the Nazis to power in 1933. The division Jewish Chaplain, Rabbi Eli Bohnen, organized the event as well as the printing of the Haggadah. "It was the first Hebrew publication in Germany since the beginning of the war," Bohnen said of the Haggadah, which means "the telling," a text that recounts the Israelites' deliverance from Egyptian bondage. It provides the structure and order of the service, written in Hebrew, held on Passover eve. "You may also be interested to learn," Bohnen said, "That the Soldiers who did the actual printing told us that when they had to clean the press before printing the Haggadah, the only rags available were some Nazi flags, which for once served a useful purpose."

Said Collins: "Fighting side by side with your Protestant and Catholic comrades, you broke into this stronghold of the tyrant, to give the lie to his rantings about the Herrenvolk (master race). You have shown by your deeds what the American Soldier can do when he fights for a cause in which he believes." Rather than the traditional concluding prayer that states "Next Year in Jerusalem," in recognition of the accomplishments of the 42nd Division, it ended with "Prayer for Home." The final song was "My Country, 'Tis of Thee". [1]

[1] https://www.dvidshub.net/news/366969/rainbow-haggadah-reminds-jewish-gis-meaning-freedom

(Above) Original Caption:
"The salute was the little Filipino lad's own idea, when a Coast Guard Combat photographer encountered him somewhere on liberated Leyte Island."

"It's parents and grandparents, spouses, children and grandchildren and other family who are protecting the home front every day. Our loved ones are why we fight."

A senior airman deployed to the farthest reaches of Asia had this to say: "There's a small bulletin board just down the hall from my deployed office that has a simple sign above it that reads, 'Why We Fight,'" she wrote. "Placed on the bulletin board are a collection of miscellaneous items put up with mismatched push-pins. One item is a desert-colored U.S. flag patch. The patch is normally worn on a desert-colored flight suit by aircrew members.

"I have no doubts that each aircrew member who wears the flag patch wears it with the utmost pride.

"All of the photos on the bulletin board of family members are those of children. The family photos show how much our military family members mean to us. They sacrifice so much every day. They give without asking for anything in return. They provide inspiration, support and love. It's parents and grandparents, spouses, children and grandchildren and other family who are protecting the home front every day. Our loved ones are why we fight.

"In the more than five months I've been deployed, no one has touched or moved them, and I highly doubt that will ever change because of their importance.

"Overall, I think everything on the 'Why We Fight' board is perfectly represented."[1]

(Right) Original Caption: "Children aboard the SS *Jean Lafitte*, bound for the States with internees freed from a Japanese internment camp in the Philippines, gather around Pendleton (Bumblebee) Thompson. Thompson volunteered as cook in the camp where they were interned."

[1] *https://www.dvidshub.net/news/50576/remember-why-we-fight-memorial-day*

"(Army) values are small town values; the way people are raised, what they believe in, and why you see those American flags along the roads."

"We talk to our soldiers every day about Army values," said the commanding general of an Army base. "They are small town values; the way people are raised, what they believe in, and why you see those American flags along the roads. It's what makes us the best Army in the world. Our soldiers live in your neighborhoods, they go to your churches, their children go to your schools, they shop in your communities. Those soldiers were in the midst of World War II, our soldiers today are just coming back from Afghanistan, Iraq and Syria. I have a great appreciation for our military, and there's nowhere else I'd rather be today than here to celebrate the men and women coming home, that have given up their time away from their Families so we could be with ours in freedom."[1]

(Right) *A U.S. Coast Guardsman visits children injured during the liberation of the Marshall Islands. Seen in the medical ward.*

[1] *https://www.dvidshub.net/news/285301/leesville-vernon-parish-open-arms-fort-polk-soldiers*

"Heroism doesn't always happen in a burst of glory. Sometimes small triumphs and large hearts change the course of history."

- *Mary Roach, author*

(This page, top and bottom) *Liberated Filipinos, 1945*

"Those who have served, whether a soldier, sailor, airman or Marine, will always be part of that great community of men and women who have put on a uniform and served this nation."

"[Soldiers are part of] the noble American tradition of (the) citizen-soldiers who embody the will of the people directly, because they are the people," said an Army general at a dedication ceremony. "Americans who serve in our military come from our local communities and return to their families in these local communities when their service has ended. (But) the U.S. Army has a saying: 'Once a soldier, a soldier for life.' This concept is shared across all our military services. Those who have served, whether a soldier, sailor, airman or Marine, will always be part of that great community of men and women who have put on a uniform and served this nation." [1]

(Left) *Generals Dwight D. Eisenhower and Omar Bradly after D-Day*

[1] *https://www.dvidshub.net/news/97952/once-soldier-soldier-life*

"As a first-generation American, the words 'independence', 'leader' and 'patriot' mean a lot to me. I've always felt these words were so special because my family escaped their country for this one. As my family celebrates 41 years here in America, I feel a renewed sense of honor to wear this uniform and a renewed sense of pride to be an American."

A Petty Officer wrote about her love of country, a story made all the more poignant because it is told from the perspective of a refugee who escaped her country for America.

"My family spent a year at the refugee camp waiting to be accepted by any government. April 30, 1980, they came to the U.S. through San Francisco.

"I lived in Rhode Island in the fifth grade, and as one of the thirteen colonies, when we learned about the American Revolution, it gave me a sense of pride and a sense of belonging -- this is my country and it's filled with patriots.

"One of those patriots, Samuel Adams, lies in an unassuming cemetery in Boston. Samuel's entire life is summed up in four roles: Signer of the Declaration of Independence, Governor of this Commonwealth, A leader of Men and an Ardent Patriot.

"As a first-generation American, the words 'independence', 'leader' and 'patriot' mean a lot to me. I've always felt these words were so special because my family escaped their country for this one.

"As my family celebrates 41 years here in America, I feel a renewed sense of honor to wear this uniform and a renewed sense of pride to be an American. I feel a sisterhood with my grandmother that crosses generations, countries and causes.

"I am proud to be a service member, a wife, a mother, a daughter, a granddaughter, a niece, Vietnamese, and a first-generation American. All these titles were given to me by the journey taken first by my grandmother all those years ago.

"By example, she taught us to be informed, to lead with compassion, and to serve those around us. I am grateful to do the same today."[1]

(Left) *A village in liberated Netherlands.*
(Right) *A Frenchman embraces a soldier after his own liberation. WWII.*

[1] *https://www.dvidshub.net/news/409568/character-man-woman-showed-me-importance-love-country*

On the eve of the Persian Gulf War (Operation Desert Storm, 1991), a British commander gave what is now a well-known speech to his troops.

"**We go to Iraq to liberate, not to conquer. We will not fly our flags in their country. We are entering Iraq to free a people, and the only flag which will be flown in that ancient land is their own. You will have to go a long way to find a more decent, generous and upright people than the Iraqis.... You will be embarrassed by their hospitality even though they have nothing. Don't treat them as refugees, for they are in their own country. Their children will be poor, in years to come they will know that the light of liberation in their lives was brought by you.**"

- *Colonel Timothy Thomas Cyril Collins OBE* [1]

[1] *https://quotepark.com/quotes/2089846-tim-collins-we-are-going-to-iraq-to-liberate-and-not-to-conque/*
[2] *https://www.dvidshub.net/news/102374/why-we-serve*

"The day we left for Kuwait was one that was rife with emotion. Although I had said my goodbyes to my friends and family well ahead of the unit's deployment ceremony, I found myself wholly unprepared for how I would feel when I saw the show of support of those who came to see us off. It was difficult to remain stoic in the face of sights such as a little girl wandering into the formation looking for "Daddy" or a coworker's wife hurrying to her husband for a last tearful embrace. I thought about all the people I saw at the ceremony throughout the whole plane ride, ruminating on the outpouring of affection that our unit received. Slowly, I am learning that any sacrifices I make are what will contribute to my goal of becoming the kind of soldier that I so admire, a soldier like my husband. Home is wherever you find yourself at the moment, and the support you seek will follow you there. Until I return to the United States, for now, I'm right at home (with my unit)."[2]

"(Serving my country) is a growing experience. It's part of growing up."

"My cousin was a Marine and was involved in the early stages of Iraq," said a Marine from Iowa. "I figured it was in my blood. I felt like I needed to become a Marine. I've always been driven to be the best, and the Marine Corps offered me the opportunity.

"I joined the Marine Corps because of 9/11, and I wanted to serve my country. It's a growing experience. It's part of growing up. It's hard coming straight out of high school and going into the adult world, especially in the military. But you learn to deal with it and take it day by day until you can see your loved ones again." The Iowan is currently on his second deployment. "This deployment is a lot more serious," he said. "It's more dangerous, this deployment. You just have to take things more seriously because you're in life and death situations out here. This deployment is a big eye opener. It's something you've been training for and preparing for the past two and half years, and it's finally happening. When you first get blown up or you first get shot at it gives a different perspective."[1]

[1] https://www.dvidshub.net/news/99062/conrad-iowa-native-serves-country-first-combat-deployment

"Military life is a very demanding life to lead. Protecting America's freedom is perhaps one of the toughest jobs."

A soldier with Multinational Force/Iraq witnessed the unearthing of the graves of about 200 men, women and children many of the victims had a single bullet wound to the head. "They were executed one by one and dumped into a large hole and buried," he said. "Over 2,000 Kurds were executed and buried in an area about half the size of a football field." Despite losing comrades and witnessing the evidence of Saddam Hussein's brutal regime, this same soldier remembered a trip to Najaf in northwestern Iraq. A group of boys was standing around as his convoy rolled up to a school. After about 15 minutes, one of the boys approached him. "I was standing in the courtyard when a young boy . . . took my hand and said, 'Thank you,'" remembered the soldier. "Not every experience over there is a bad one. For every shooting or death or injury, there's a little girl high-fiving soldiers and Marines, or a new Iraqi soldier making a decent living and providing for his family. Or better yet, there is a brand-new country being stood up, saved from tyranny and introduced to democracy."

"I was blessed to be born in the United States and be known in history as an American soldier."[2]

He thought about that a moment, then continued: "The American public needs to take just a minute to say thank you to a veteran," he said. "Not only on Veterans Day, but every day. These men and women sacrificed themselves so that Americans can be free. It doesn't really matter if they served overseas or domestically, because military life is a very demanding life to lead. Protecting America's freedom is perhaps one of the toughest jobs, and it takes much courage and dedication to do so."[1]

(Facing page) Liberated Iraq. **(This page)** Afghanistan evacuation, 2021.

[1] https://www.dvidshub.net/news/3707/veterans-day-has-fresh-meaning-iraqi-freedom-vets
[2] https://www.dvidshub.net/news/101756/why-we-serve-sgt-tad-randell

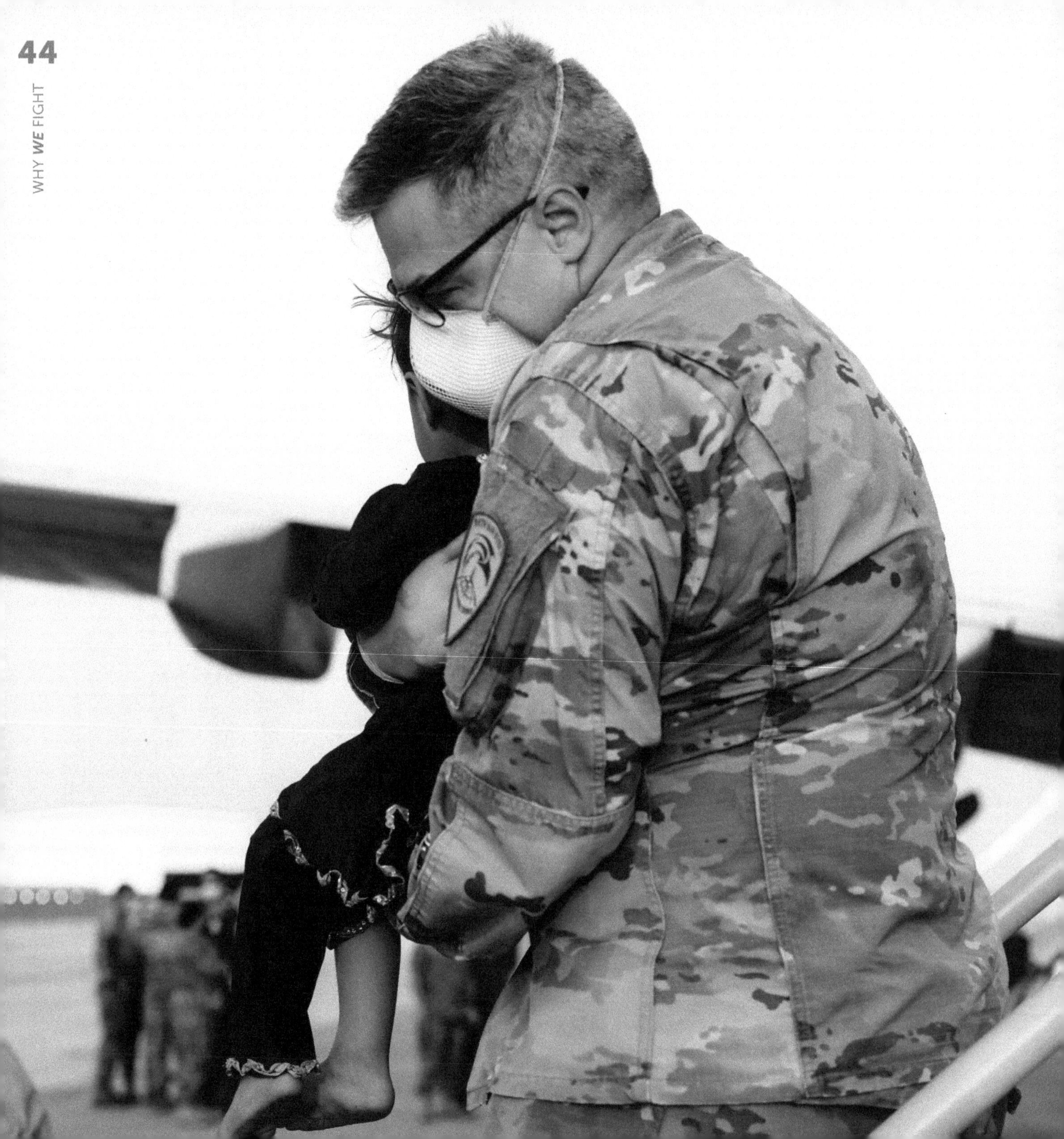

"If I can do my job right," said a combat medic who served in Afghanistan, "when my kids walk across that stage to receive their high school diploma and a recruiter asks if they want to serve, they can say, 'Thanks, but my dad has done enough serving for all of us.' (My grandfather) inspired me to believe that every able body should enlist once in the military. If everyone enlisted, then people in this country would be more appreciative and proud of a country that, I believe, God allowed them to be born in."[1]

(All Photos, both pages) Scenes from the Afghanistan evacuation, 2021, and from Operation Iraqi Freedom

[1] https://www.dvidshub.net/news/101756/why-we-serve-sgt-tad-randell

"The price of freedom is eternal vigilance."

- Phil Plait, author

"After doing what I had done, and seen what I've seen, you start to put things into perspective," said one sergeant after his deployment to Operation Iraqi Freedom. "Words such as honor, virtue, and pride, I've learned, still have tangible meaning. You see it heavily represented in shows and movies about soldiers who served in World War II. That same pride is still alive today.

"I have traveled all over the world, but there is nowhere on this planet I would rather be than in the United States. Where else can you find a place where a man can start off with nothing and end up with everything? That's the American dream.

"I've made the commitment to lay my life on the line for my country, and I'll be doing that until the day I die," he concluded. "I believe this country was founded on the principles of God. I could've been born anywhere else, but I was blessed to be born in the United States and be known in history as an American soldier."[1]

(This page): *Army helicopter pilots move to forward NATO bases during 2022 Ukraine crisis.*
(Facing page): *Scenes from Afghanistan evacuation*

[1] *https://www.dvidshub.net/news/101756/why-we-serve-sgt-tad-randell*

"**Our policy is not against any country or doctrine, but against hunger, poverty, desperation, and chaos. Its purpose should be the arrival of a working economy in the world so as to permit the emergence of political and social conditions in which free institutions can exist.**"

- General George Marshall

"I have come to realize that if you have the opportunity to do something, you should just go do it, especially given our jobs - we never know when there is going to be a major event we will have to react to. I don't want to look back and say, 'I wish I would have.'"[1]

(**All Photos, both pages**) *Scenes from Afghanistan evacuation, 2021, and from Operation Iraqi Freedom*

[1] *https://www.dvidshub.net/news/100572/soldier-finds-strength-through-loved-aunts-memory*

"I know I wouldn't be happy not wearing this uniform."[1]

"When you go somewhere where people aren't really familiar with the military, they appreciate you so much. It's like -- they see this uniform as a beacon. When I got home after Iraq, little kids came up to me and although they didn't understand what I had done, they knew who I was, and that is what keeps me serving."[2]

"I only hope that any help I give makes someone else's day not as difficult as the day before," said a Marine Corps corporal. "There is more to life than just yourself."[3]

[1] https://www.dvidshub.net/news/149395/marine-sergeant-battles-back-brain-cancer-return-active-duty

[2] https://www.dvidshub.net/news/100572/soldier-finds-strength-through-loved-aunts-memory

[3] https://www.dvidshub.net/news/122839/helping-others-help-herself-spouse-selflessly-dedicates-help-others

"All of my grandparents were Marines," said a 22-year-old Marine Corps Corporal deployed to Afghanistan. "Pretty much my entire family was in the service. When I was little, all my friends wanted to play dress up as princesses or ballerinas. I wanted to play dress up in my grandmother's old uniform." Like many service men and women, this Marine joined straight out of high school and is now part of a larger Marine family. She is married to a Marine and has five relatives who are Marines. "I never really thought of it as a tradition," she said in an interview. "But I have little brothers who already want to join, and I imagine that when I have children, they'll probably want to join, too. I've had a great Marine Corps career so far. I couldn't imagine doing anything else after high school. I love being able to experience the culture and also being able to help with humanitarian assistance and aid."[1]

"To me, the American Dream means that I can dream," said Staff Sgt. Laura Mardukhayeva, a Russian emigree who in 2021 volunteered to assist Afghan nationals transitioning to life in the United States. "It doesn't mean a white picket fence. It means that we get to choose what our fence looks like."[2]

[1] https://www.dvidshub.net/news/84509/tennessee-marine-continues-family-legacy-afghanistan

[2] Quoted in DVIDS, Story by Sgt. Marc Loi, "Task Force Spartan" dateline KUWAIT11.01.2021

"You've given up the comforts of home, the tranquility of civilian life, and left your family, friends and the American public behind to come out and try to end another war."

(This page and facing page) *Sailors man the rails as they arrive in port*

Said a Petty Officer on the aircraft carrier USS Dwight D. Eisenhower, speaking at his ship's program to honor Veteran's Day: "You are that special breed of American who, as Abraham Lincoln once said, stands ready to 'lay so costly a sacrifice upon the altar of Freedom.' You've given up the comforts of home, the tranquility of civilian life, and left your family, friends and the American public behind to come out and try to end another war. Never forget you are that one percent, the ones in uniform with incredible skill, discipline and invaluable leadership. Indeed, American veterans remain some of the most talented, driven and capable people on earth. While average 20-something American youth are still finding their place in the world, 20-something veterans are leading sailors, adapting to unpredictably, operating cutting-edge technology, performing under pressure, rebuilding towns and mediating tribal disputes. In short, you get it done, you are selfless, you are brave, and you remain the backbone of America."[1]

"I think of a hero as someone who understands the degree of responsibility that comes with his freedom."

- Bob Dylan

[1] https://www.dvidshub.net/news/219197/historians-reflection-veterans-day

"As I drove through base that night, I tried to remember why exactly I decided to become a full-time Airman. It's often said that it's the people, not the aircraft, that make the Air Force great. It can be a cliché, to be sure, but it is true from an operations standpoint, and even when I put the mission aside and look at it from my own personal experiences as a junior enlisted Airman, I believe that sentiment to be true wholeheartedly. Thank you to everyone who came before me and everyone who serves with me today. You are what makes the rollercoaster ride of triumph and struggle that is the military worth it for me. You convinced me to take the leap and leave my plan behind to pursue a higher calling. You are why I consider it to be one of the utmost

(Photos) *Evacuation of Afghanistan, 2021*

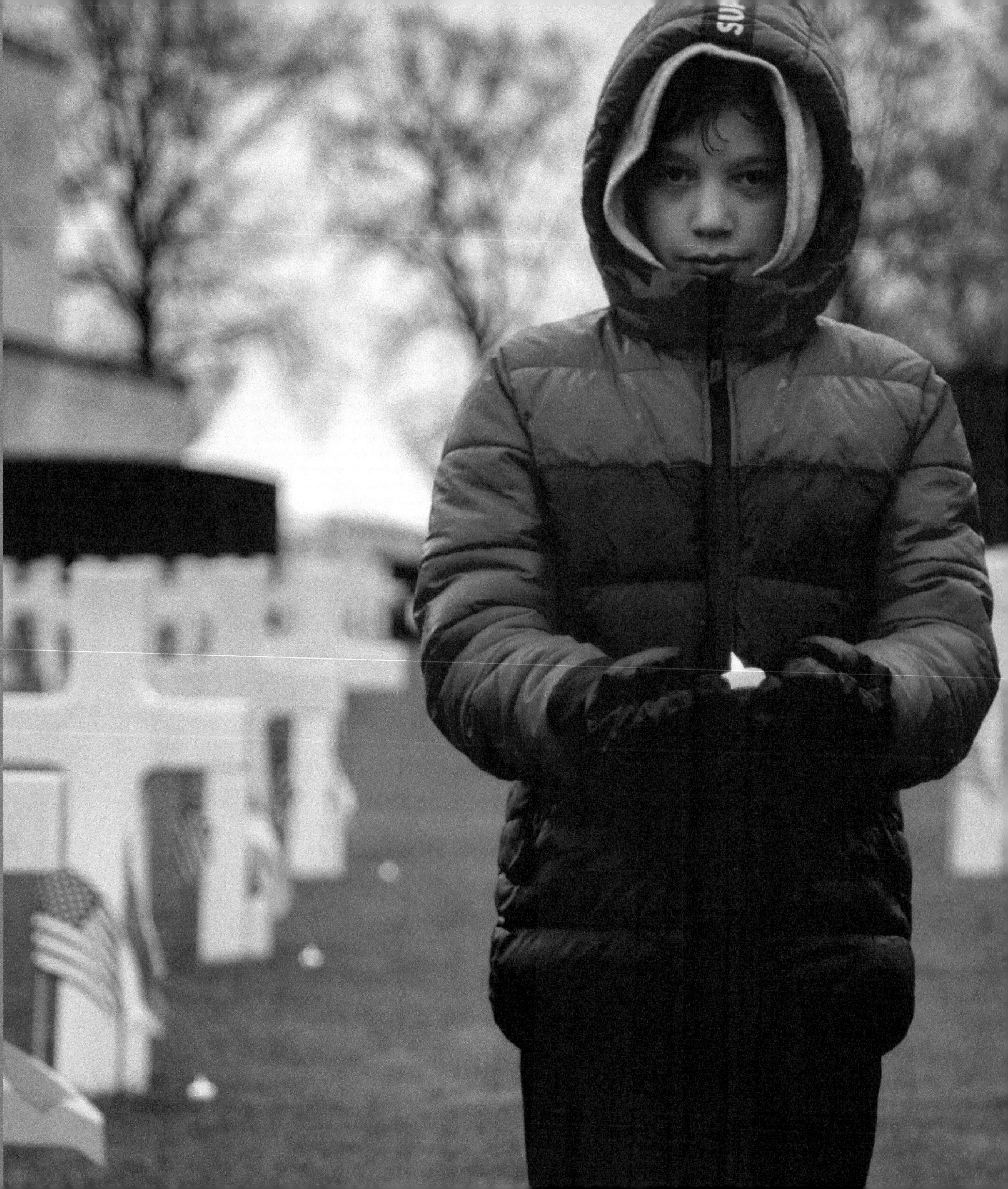

"I'm just glad to have done something," said an Army sergeant of his tour in Afghanistan. "I was 24 and working at a gas station. I wasn't really doing much with my life. Joining the Army was always something I wanted to do. After years of seeing the war go on, I didn't want to grow old and not be able to tell my grandchildren I participated in this. It would have upset me. I was feeling like I was sitting on the sidelines when our country was doing something like this." He joined and was deployed to Afghanistan. He lost nine friends from his platoon. Still, he reenlisted. "I was thinking about getting out after the last deployment, but I didn't want to give up after these guys gave it their all. They lost their lives doing something they believed in and I think it would have tore me up the rest of my life if I would have just stopped and not come back here …(Their memory) reminds me of why I'm here."[1]

(Left) *A young boy poses with a tea light during the Luxembourg American Cemetery Luminary event, at Luxembourg American Cemetery, Luxembourg Dec. 13, 2019. The Luminary gives service members and civilians the opportunity to display the enduring commitment to remembering the fallen by placing tea lights at each of the headstones.* **(U.S. Air Force photo by Senior Airman Deven Schultz)**

[1] *https://www.dvidshub.net/news/60117/no-slack-soldier-no-stranger-afghanistan*

"The patriot's blood is the seed of Freedom's tree."

- Thomas Campbell, Revolutionary War poet

"It makes sense what we did on Iwo Jima. Taking Iwo Jima saved a lot of air lives."

"I was in the sixth wave in," said a WWII vet on the battle for Iwo Jima. "My job was to take the half-tracks up the front line and find out where they were supposed to be, and then get them into place. I was in a foxhole when the flag was raised. All of a sudden, I hear the ships out in the harbor start tooting their horns. Then people started saying, 'Look at Suribachi!' Taking Mount Suribachi and raising the flag was the biggest success of that operation. When I was on there fighting, I began to wonder what we were fighting for. It's a lousy, stinkin' volcanic island. Later on, I was at a banquet in Dallas and I was walking past a table and a guy grabs me and said, 'You saved my life!' He said, 'I landed the first B-29 plane on Iwo Jima.' Then it makes sense what we did on Iwo Jima. Taking Iwo Jima saved a lot of air lives, more lives than we lost, more planes and equipment, too. Taking the island was one big victory in the war. I was on Iwo Jima for 45 days. I didn't get injured or anything, and I owe it to three things: I prayed hard, I dug deep, and I ran fast."[1]

[1] https://www.dvidshub.net/news/155929/reflections-iwo-jima-sergeant-william-bill-schott-prayed-hard-dug-deep-and-ran-fast

"It reminds me that there (are) always so many people behind us, supporting us, (who) think everything of us, of what we do."

"You come across people in the Airport who say, 'Thank you for your service, thank you for your support,'" said a newly minted, 19-year-old Army private. "Seeing the elementary (school) kids kind of look at us in awe, the ones in uniform and just single us out as heroes at such a young age, it's an incredible feeling: It reminds me that there (are) always so many people behind us, supporting us, (who) think everything of us, of what we do."[1]

(This page, top): *Families watch as soldiers deploy to Europe during the Russian invasion of Ukraine.*
(Bottom): *A soldier comforts a child during the evacuation of Afghanistan.*

[1] https://www.dvidshub.net/news/113242/kentuckians-honor-cost-freedom-labor-day-weekend

Navy Adm. Mike Mullen, then Chairman of the Joint Chefs of Staff, addressed the forces of the United States military. "History teaches us that peace does not preserve itself. It demands effort and pain and sacrifice. It also requires generations of young men and women willing to deploy to the far ends of the earth to, as one memorial puts it, defend countries 'they never knew and a people they never met.' Today, a new generation of GI's has deployed to far-off places and defend people they did not know. War has bloodied them. Loss has tempered them. Great families have sustained them. Through it all, they have emerged the most resilient, combat-ready force I have seen in my four decades of service. And yet, they continue to look to veterans past - their predecessors — and they know they stand on very broad shoulders."[1]

[1] https://www.dvidshub.net/news/59852/chairmans-corner-happy-veterans-day

"We can only know what we are
to do in life after we know what story
of which we are a part."

- Alastair McIntyre, British philosopher

"The next generation of our country is in good hands," said a Texas soldier of the elementary school he visited. "They're being brought up the way they need to, to carry on the freedoms we hold dear. They understand what freedom means. They truly ... understand their choice for education and religion and the freedoms that they have. They seem very, very gracious to have that freedom."[1]

[1] *https://www.dvidshub.net/news/56237/1st-air-cav-kids-celebrate-freedom*

"I can only rest for a moment, for with freedom comes responsibilities, and I dare not linger."

"I have walked that long road to freedom. I have tried not to falter; I have made missteps along the way. But I have discovered the secret that after climbing a great hill, one only finds that there are many more hills to climb. I have taken a moment here to rest, to steal a view of the glorious vista that surrounds me, to look back on the distance I have come.
But I can only rest for a moment, for with freedom comes responsibilities, and I dare not linger, for my long walk is not ended."

- Nelson Mandela

Douglas Keeney

is the author of bestselling books on events that shaped American and world history including *The Eleventh Hour*, *15 Minutes* and, most recently, *The Lives They Saved: Medics, Mariners and the Boatlift That Saved 260,000 On 9.11*. Keeney's books have been well reviewed by *The New York Times*, *The Wall Street Journal*, *The New Yorker*, *Slate*, *Newsweek* and numerous other publications. He has appeared on Fox TV, PBS, The Learning Channel and other broadcast outlets and he works extensively with all of the branches of the U.S. military as both a researcher and an author. Keeney is the cofounder of The Military Channel (now American Heroes) and is a frequent keynote speaker. He has held his pilot license for 25 years, is an avid tennis player and a scuba diver. He is married to the journalist Jill Johnson Keeney, with whom they have two sons

CPSIA information can be obtained
at www.ICGtesting.com
Printed in the USA
JSHW061138110622
26969JS00004B/2